Size of the Problem

DINOSAUR BIRTHDAY PARTY

Think Social Publishing, Inc., Santa Clara, California

www.socialthinking.com

Size of the Problem
Dinosaur Birthday Party

Ryan Hendrix, Kari Zweber Palmer, Nancy Tarshis, Michelle Garcia Winner

ISBN: 978-1-936943-33-3

Think Social Publishing, Inc.
404 Saratoga Avenue, Suite 200
Santa Clara, CA 95050
Tel: (408) 557-8595
Fax: (408) 557-8594

This book was printed and bound in the United States by Mighty Color Printing.
Think Social Publishing is a sole source provider.
Books may be purchased online at www.socialthinking.com.

Introduction to Storybook ⑨

In-the-moment problem solving is a complex process! In this storybook we define a problem as something that happens that was not part of the plan AND makes people feel uncomfortable. Our goal for this unit is to raise our students' awareness of four key concepts that help our students learn to self-regulate as they work through their problems: 1) problems come in different sizes; 2) feelings and emotional reactions come in different sizes; 3) reactions come from feelings, and 4) it is expected to match the size of our reaction to the size of the problem. These concepts all work together and contribute to us solving our personal and social problems.

We Thinkers! Our Amazing Early Learner Curriculum!

We Thinkers! Volume 1* - *Social Explorers* and Volume 2 - *Social Problem Solvers* is an engaging Social Thinking® series designed to teach Michelle Garcia Winner's basic Social Thinking Vocabulary concepts to children ages 4-7. Each volume consists of storybooks, curricula and kid-friendly music that make core social concepts come alive for young learners. The teaching is cumulative: Volume 1 helps prime students for the deeper social concepts and activities in Volume 2.

Volume 1 explores five basic social concepts that help children learn to think about others as they learn to be part of a group: *thinking thoughts and feeling feelings, the group plan, thinking with your eyes, body in the group, and whole body listening.* Volume 2 introduces five core Social Thinking concepts related to teaching stronger executive functioning in a classroom or group setting: *hidden rules and expected/ unexpected behavior, making a smart guess, flexible versus stuck thinking, the size of a problem, and sharing an imagination.* Each storybook is aligned with a curriculum unit that breaks down these social emotional concepts into concrete, teachable segments. Adults find detailed strategies and explicit ways to engage students and foster deeper learning about each concept.

Our goal in developing the *We Thinkers!* series is to provide sequenced clear instruction to engage students in their own social emotional learning so they can become better group collaborators and problem solvers. To that end, in Volume 2 we introduce a Group Collaboration, Play and Problem Solving (GPS) scale, checklist and interactive play activities. These materials guide parents and professionals in evaluating each child's current abilities to relate to their peers and then choose from an array of interactive play activities based on their particular social learning needs.

While all children can benefit from the social emotional teaching that is at the foundation of our *We Thinkers!* series, it was specifically designed to help promote social learning in children who have solid to strong language and academic learning skills who also have social learning challenges (e.g. autism spectrum levels 1 and 2, ADHD, social communication or anxiety disorders, etc. or no diagnoses). However, mainstream teachers now adopt our materials for use with all students as they find them user-friendly for all.

* formerly titled *The Incredible Flexible You, Volume 1*

Teaching the Curriculum, Concepts and Activities

What does play have to do with group collaboration and classroom learning? It is well documented in the research that interactive and pretend play is the avenue through which our young children practice and perfect their social thinking and social skills. By the time children enter kindergarten it is assumed they have learned basic concepts and skills that allow them to work and learn academic concepts in a group setting.

It's tempting to think of play as simple, but it's actually a highly complex array of concepts and skills that work together simultaneously to enable a child to be successful in playing and interacting with others. Through interactive play children learn pivotal group interaction skills that will carry them through to adulthood. Play encourages the development of problem solving and conflict resolution skills, facilitates central thinking, conceptual development, perspective taking, and executive functioning.

Our multi-sensory curriculum reflects the idea that learning should be interactive and playful. Activities involve using our eyes, ears, body and brain to make important social emotional connections. Teaching within the series draws on:

- "bibliotherapy" – using the words and illustrations in storybooks to help young learners develop an understanding of self and others and elicit a therapeutic response;

- "music therapy" – using music to help foster engagement around our core social emotional concepts;

- a wide range of activities to encourage children to explore and practice each of our 10 core concepts;

- "differentiated interactive play instruction" – not all children have the same abilities to play with other children. Through our GPS scale and checklist, parents and professionals can select which play activities are best suited to the child's level.

Together, the materials provided in our *We Thinkers!* series help young learners develop the five core competencies at the heart of social and emotional learning (SEL): self-awareness, self-management, social awareness, relationship skills, and responsible decision-making. The concepts marry playful, interactive learning to Common Core, state or country standards of education around the world.

Pace Yourself and Your Kids!

The concepts in Volume 2 explore group collaboration at a deeper level and the ideas are a little more detailed to teach. To increase engagement and protect kids from becoming overwhelmed, we recommend teaching the stories in sections. While we encourage you to let your students guide you in determining the "best" places to start and stop, we've noticed in our own "test teaching" more natural breaking points in the plot and content. These sections are outlined below and are marked in the story.

Section 1, pages 1-6: Define the concepts: problem, reaction
Introduce: problems come in all sizes; we try to match our reaction to the size of the problem

Section 2, pages 7-15: Define small problems and discuss reactions to small problems

Section 3, pages 16-26: Define medium problems and discuss reactions to medium sized problems

Section 4, pages 27-33: Define big problems and discuss reactions to big problems

Section 5, pages 34-36: Showing small reactions to small problems keeps the party going!

The *We Thinkers!* series is available for purchase in the U.S. at www.socialthinking.com.

Today is Jesse's birthday! Evan, Ellie and Molly are coming to his apartment for his birthday party. All of their dinosaur friends are invited too. Before everyone arrives, Jesse and his family are busy getting ready for the party.

As Jesse helps his dad frost the cake, he leans in too close.
Oh no! There is frosting all over his shirt.

Jesse has a **problem**. A problem is something that happens that is NOT
part of the plan and makes a person have uncomfortable feelings.
The plan was to frost the cake, NOT to frost his shirt.

When a problem happens, you can have a lot of different thoughts and feelings on the inside. Your reaction is what you show on the outside, by how you look, what you do, and what you say.

Jesse getting frosting on his shirt is a small problem. Jesse feels a little disappointed because he wanted to wear it to the party.

Jesse stays calm. He has a calm face, a calm body, and uses a calm voice. "I'll be right back, Dad," Jesse says. Then he goes to change into another shirt.

Jesse is showing a small reaction to his problem. Everyone feels comfortable that Jesse is showing a small reaction to his small problem and that he has an idea about how to solve his problem. Jesse feels good too.

Jesse changes his shirt just in time for his friends to arrive. "Happy birthday," they all say as Jesse opens the door. The kids are excited to celebrate with Jesse and Jesse is so glad they can be there. Their dinosaur friends will arrive soon. The kids love to play with their dinosaur friends. But they also know that some problems will happen. That's expected! When the dinosaurs come over, there are *always* problems.

Stop and Discuss

Dinosaurs come in all different sizes and so do problems!

Some dinosaurs are small and some problems are small.

Some dinosaurs are medium size and some problems are medium.

Some dinosaurs are big and some problems are big!

Stop and Notice

The small dinosaurs arrive first. Oops! One knocks streamers down with his tail. Another accidentally rips the wrapping paper off a gift, and a third bumps into Evan. That wasn't part of the plan. Now there are some problems.

These are small problems. They can be taken care of quickly and with just a little help from others. It's expected that people stay pretty calm when small problems happen. That keeps everyone feeling comfortable.

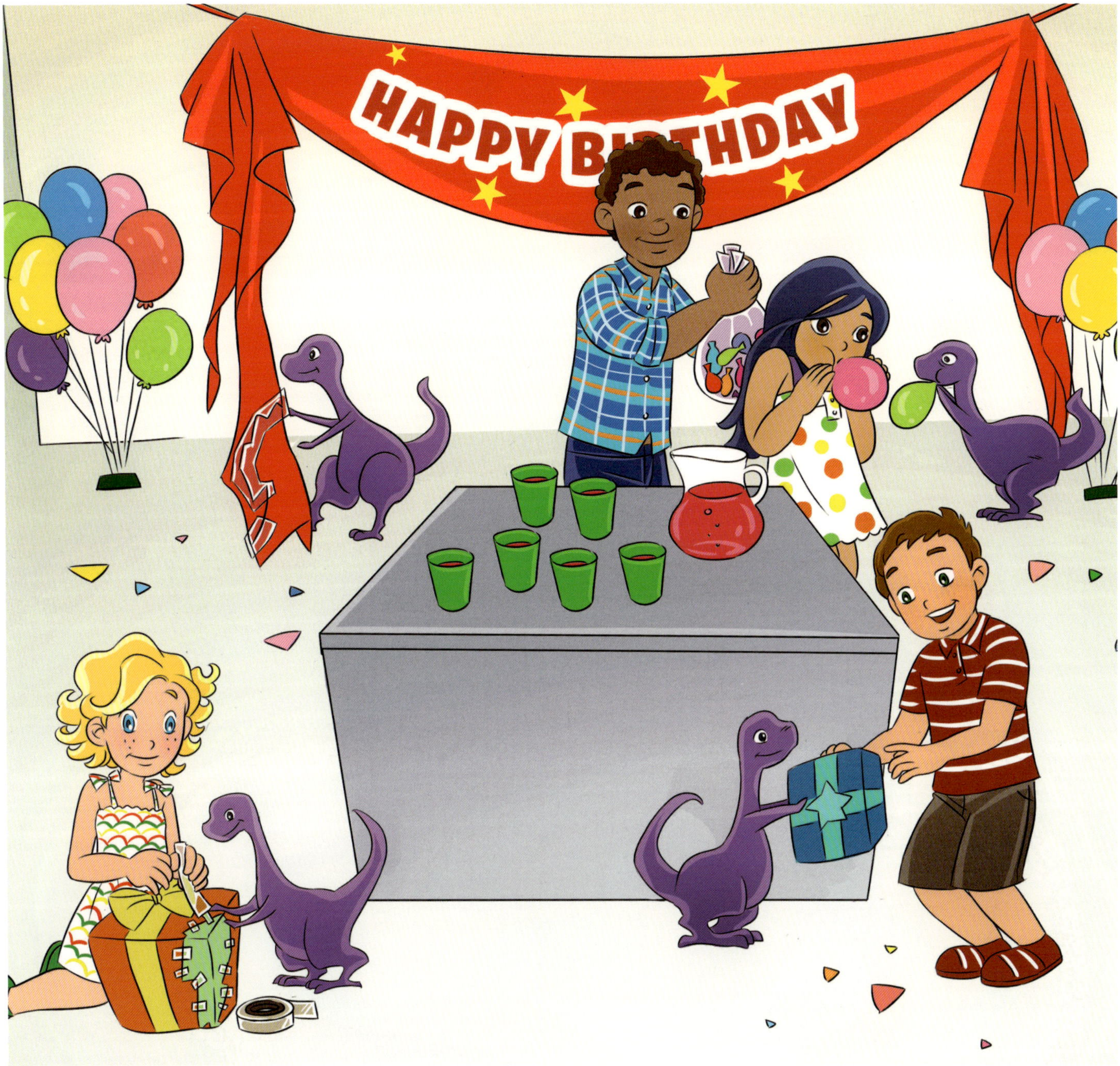
HAPPY BIRTHDAY

"Oops, the wrapping paper is torn," Ellie says to the dinosaur, "I'll help you tape it back on!"

"That's okay," Jesse says to the dinosaur that popped the balloon.

"We can just blow up more," offers Molly.

"I know that was an accident," Evan says as he smiles at the small dinosaur that bumped into him.

Everyone stays calm and the problems are solved quickly.

Stop and Notice

Oops! Another small problem happens when a dinosaur knocks over Ellie's drink. Spilling a drink is a small problem. Ellie and the dinosaur can fix it quickly by wiping it up.

Everyone is showing small reactions... except Ellie. She feels angry and is crying. She is having a big reaction to a small problem. That's unexpected. Ellie's big reaction makes the dinosaurs and kids feel uncomfortable.

Ellie's reaction does not match the size of the problem.

Spilling a drink is a small problem.

Yelling and crying is a BIG reaction.

Stop and Notice

Ellie notices the dinosaur is wiping up the spill. "Oh, this is just a small problem," she thinks. She calms down, gets a new drink, and the dinosaur helps clean up the mess!

When problems are small, like spilling a drink, and people stay calm, this helps fix the problem quickly. That's expected. Everyone feels good.

When the reaction matches the size of the problem, everyone feels calm and comfortable and the fun continues. Spilling the drink was a small problem and now Ellie is showing a small reaction.

Stop and Notice

Ellie helps herself to a snack and...uh oh! She knocks over her drink!

This time Ellie makes a different choice. She stops and thinks to herself, "This is just a small problem, I can stay calm. When I stay calm I will feel better and other people will feel good too." Then she quickly wipes up the spill.

Ellie's small reaction to the small problem makes everyone feel comfortable. Ellie feels proud that she was flexible, showed a small reaction to the small problem, and made the problem better on her own.

Next, the medium-sized dinosaurs arrive. Uh oh! One steps on a gift and breaks the toy inside. Another sits on a chair and it breaks too. A third accidently knocks over a lamp. That wasn't part of the plan and now there are medium problems.

Medium problems take a while to fix and most are too hard for kids and dinosaurs to fix themselves. It's expected that people feel upset when medium problems happen.

But, the kids know they can make these problems better. They will need glue, a hammer and nails, a light bulb, and grown-ups! Jesse's parents hear noises and come to see what is going on. Adults have more practice staying calm with medium problems. They ask, "What happened?"

The kids and dinosaurs take a deep breath, calm down, and ask Jesse's parents for help. They all work together and everyone feels better.

Uh oh… another medium problem happens when a dinosaur takes a bite out of Jesse's birthday cake. The kids all feel surprised and upset. The dinosaur is sad and worried about how Jesse will feel. Everyone is showing medium reactions… except Evan. He thinks the dinosaur ruined the cake and feels REALLY MAD. Evan is showing a BIG reaction. He yells, he screams, he cries. That's unexpected. Even Jesse understands it is a medium problem and knows the dinosaur did not mean to cause a problem.

Evan's reaction does not match the size of the problem.
Taking a big bite out of the cake is a medium problem. Crying, yelling,
and pounding on the ground is a BIG reaction.

The kids will need help and more time to fix this medium problem. They talk with Jesse's parents about different ideas to make this problem better.

"Maybe we should throw the cake away," says Molly.

"The dinosaur didn't lick all of the cake," says Jesse, "and I think we have leftover frosting."

They make a plan to cut away the part of the cake the dinosaur was munching on and add more frosting to the cake that is left.

Once Evan understands the new group plan, he figures out this is a medium-sized problem. This helps Evan feel calm again and he helps Jesse and Molly fix the cake. This makes everyone feel good. Jesse tells Evan and Molly, "There will also be chocolate chip ice cream to eat!"

Stop and Discuss

Uh oh! While they were frosting the cake, the dinosaur *ate* the ice cream! Ice cream is everywhere and the dinosaur ate almost all of it. There will be no ice cream with the cake. This is a medium-sized problem.

The kids feel really disappointed.

Chocolate chip is Evan's favorite flavor of ice cream and now there isn't any to eat. He feels upset but he shows a medium-sized reaction to this medium problem.

The kids ask Jesse's parents about getting more ice cream. "Sorry kids," they answer, "there is no time to go and get more, so there will be no ice cream at the party." They kids all feel upset. They stop and think about what would happen if they have big reactions.

Evan thinks about how the dinosaur would feel if he shouted at him and made angry fists.

Jesse imagines himself furiously jumping and Ellie thinks about herself yelling.

When Molly has big reactions she cries, takes her body out of the group, or says nothing at all.

None of these reactions would make ANYONE feel good and they would not make the problem better.

If they get stuck on the idea of eating ice cream or if they have big reactions, they will feel really bad, others will be uncomfortable, and they won't be able to have as much fun at Jesse's party.

Not all problems can be fixed and not all problems have to be fixed.

Sometimes you just have to be flexible and move on with the plan.

We call this *letting it go*.

"This is just a medium problem," thinks Jesse.

"The party is not about the ice cream! We can have a party without it,"
Evan tells himself.

"Not getting to eat ice cream is not a big problem," Molly thinks.

"If I can let it go, I will have more fun," thinks Ellie.

They all take a deep breath, think flexibly, and choose to let the problem go.

The fun continues! This makes everyone feel good.

Everyone is ready to play *Pin the Tail On the Dinosaur* while they wait for
the big dinosaur to arrive. It's Jesse's turn when suddenly they hear
a huge CRASH! What was that?

Stop and Discuss

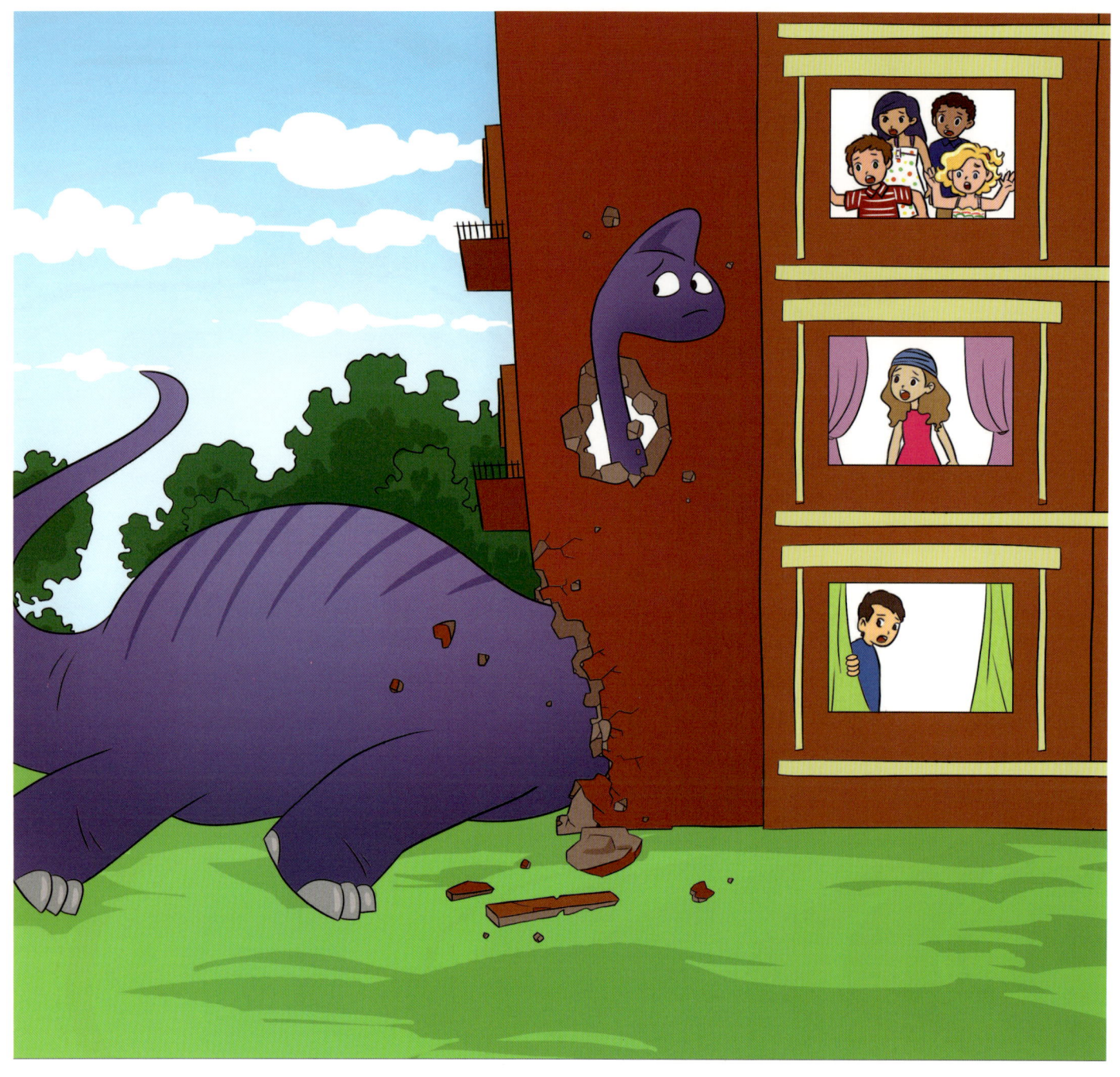

YIKES! The big dinosaur is stuck in the building! That wasn't part of the plan... and now there is a BIG problem. They feel worried and scared about what will happen to the big dinosaur and to the building. Everyone has big reactions. They cry and yell. They have to call for help because this problem is bigger than any of them can handle!

Getting stuck in the building is a BIG problem because it will take a lot of help from a lot of people and a lot of time to make it better. It is expected that people have big reactions to BIG problems. Even adults may have big reactions to big problems!

Stop and Notice

Many different adults come together to try and help!

They try lots of different ideas and plans to solve this BIG problem.

The kids calm down and help think about a solution. They decide to try
another way to get the dinosaur out of the building and use the
extra frosting to make her slippery and slide her out.
They all work together and finally she is free!

The group needs to change the plan.

They want to finish the party, but the big dinosaur can't get into the building. Jesse thinks about his favorite place, the playground in the park. Then he thinks about dinosaurs on the playground and all the problems that could happen since the slide, swings, and sandbox are not set up for dinosaurs!

Jesse thinks of another idea—they can go to the open field in the park instead of the playground! Everyone agrees and sets off for the field.

The kids are having a great time playing at the field.

Some problems happen, but that's expected.

Jesse is so excited about his new airplane toy that he doesn't share it
with his dinosaur friend.

Evan and another dinosaur want to play different games. Molly forgot her
party hat at the apartment and is disappointed she can't wear it.

Ellie wants to play *Pin the Tail On the Dinosaur* but the line is so long!

Jesse makes a smart guess that the dinosaur wants a turn and thinks, "I can share my toy." Evan and the dinosaur are flexible and take turns playing each other's games. Molly and the dinosaur trade hats.

Ellie wants her turn. She stops and thinks, "Waiting is a small problem. If I wait, others will feel comfortable, we can keep playing, and that will be fun!"

Stop and Discuss

Jesse is so happy to be with all of his friends. He thinks that this party was not what was planned at all, but it's the best party ever!

Happy birthday Jesse, happy birthday to you!